PAUL & YOLANDA

FINANCIAL PLANNING GUIDE for YOUR MONEY MATTERS

FINANCIAL PLANNING GUIDE for YOUR MONEY MATTERS

Malcolm MacGregor

UPDATED EDITION
1981

BETHANY HOUSE PUBLISHERS
MINNEAPOLIS, MINNESOTA 55438
A Division of Bethany Fellowship, Inc.

Financial Planning Guide
for Your Money Matters

Malcolm MacGregor

ISBN 0-87123-166-2

Published by Bethany Fellowship, Inc.
6820 Auto Club Road, Minneapolis, Minnesota, 55438

Printed in the United States of America

Contents

Preface

This Planning Guide is divided into sections as follows:

SECTION 1 *Biblical Principles of Personal Finance*
An alphabetical listing of major themes with scripture references to allow you to see what the Bible has to say about the subject.

SECTION 2 *Home Budget*
A simple yet efficient budgeting system with easy-to-follow examples. The use of this system will enable you to plan for and gain financial freedom.

SECTION 3 *Seminar Study Guide*
An outline of the major points and scriptures shared in the Money Matters Seminar. This can be used in a live teaching, along with the Money Matters cassette album, or as a self-study guide.

SECTION 4 *Practical Applications*
A list of many ideas to help you in saving money in all areas of your shopping. Additionally there is a series of listings for permanent recording of your assets and important papers. Finally, a family information packet to aid you in preparing your family will.

This planning guide can be used only as a tool for budget preparation or as a study aid in understanding God's approach to your money. To get maximum benefit from your study, I suggest you get a copy of the tape cassette album, *Your Money Matters*. The album can be ordered through your local Christian bookstore, a Successful Living Dealer in your area, Bethany Fellowship, or through me at the address listed under A Final Note on page 36.

OTHER MATERIALS AVAILABLE

Your Money Matters—tape cassette album $29.95
Building the Temple—cassette teaching—a church involved in a building program 4.95
Your Money Matters—book 3.95
Training Your Children to Handle Money—book 3.95
Financial Planning Guide/with cassette tape 9.95
God's Purpose for the Christian Businessman—tape cassette album 24.95

SECTION 1

Biblical Principles of Personal Finances

Accounting
Daniel 6:1-3
Matthew 18:23
Matthew 25:14-30
Romans 14:12

Attitudes Towards Others—Their Consequences

Helping the Poor
Psalms 69:33
Psalms 72:12-14
Psalms 109:31
Proverbs 14:21
Proverbs 14:31
Matthew 5:42
Matthew 6:19-20
Matthew 10:42
Luke 3:11
Luke 9:48
Luke 10:35
Luke 12:33
Luke 19:8, 9
1 Timothy 5:3, 5, 8, 16

Against the Poor
Deuteronomy 24:14
Psalms 10:2
Psalms 12:5
Proverbs 14:20, 21, 31
Proverbs 21:13
Proverbs 22:16
Proverbs 24:23
Proverbs 28:8
Matthew 18:23-34
Luke 11:42
Luke 16:19-25

Favoring the Wealthy
Deuteronomy 1:17
Deuteronomy 16:19
Proverbs 14:20
Proverbs 28:21
Romans 12:16

Budgeting and Planning
Proverbs 16:9
Proverbs 19:21
Proverbs 22:3
Proverbs 24:3, 4
Proverbs 27:12
Luke 12:16-21
Luke 14:28-30
Luke 14:28-30
Luke 16:1-8
1 Corinthians 16:1, 2

Business

Attitudes and Actions
Leviticus 19:12
Psalms 112
Proverbs 10:4

Proverbs 13:4
Proverbs 13:11
Proverbs 24:10
Proverbs 28:27
Ecclesiastes 5:12
Malachi 3:5
Luke 6:35a
Romans 12:11
Ephesians 4:28

Honesty vs. Unjust Gain
Deuteronomy 25:15
Proverbs 11:1
Proverbs 16:8
Proverbs 22:16
Proverbs 28:8
Jeremiah 22:13
Luke 16:10
Romans 12:17

Contentment
Joshua 7:7
Proverbs 30:7-9
Luke 3:14
Luke 12:15-21
2 Corinthians 6:10
Philippians 4:11, 12
1 Timothy 6:6-10
Hebrews 13:5

Cosigning Notes
Proverbs 6:1-5
Proverbs 11:15
Proverbs 17:18
Proverbs 20:16
Proverbs 22:26
Proverbs 27:13

Covetousness
Psalms 73:2-3
Psalms 73:13, 17, 20
Proverbs 23:4-5
Luke 12:15
Luke 18:10-14
Luke 18:24
Ephesians 5:5

Debt
Deuteronomy 15:6
Deuteronomy 28:12, 13
2 Kings 4:1
Psalms 37:21
Proverbs 3:27, 28
Proverbs 6:1-3
Proverbs 11:15
Proverbs 17:18
Proverbs 22:7
Proverbs 27:13
Matthew 5:25, 26
Matthew 18:23
Luke 12:58, 59
Romans 13:8

Discipline
Matthew 7:13, 14
Luke 9:51
2 Corinthians 8:11
2 Thessalonians 3:11
Hebrews 12:11

Dishonesty
Psalms 37:37
Psalms 62:10-12
Proverbs 10:15, 16
Proverbs 11:16, 18
Proverbs 12:3, 12
Proverbs 13:7
Proverbs 15:27

Proverbs 20:21
Proverbs 22:28
Proverbs 24:19-20
Proverbs 28:22
Matthew 18:7
Matthew 27:5
Luke 9:25
Luke 11:42
Luke 16:1, 11, 12, 13
Luke 20:46-47
Romans 2:21-22

Facts
Proverbs 14:8, 15
Proverbs 18:13
Proverbs 19:2
Proverbs 23:23
Proverbs 27:23, 24
Luke 14:31, 32
James 1:5

Hoarding
Psalms 49:11
Psalms 49:16-17
Proverbs 13:22
Malachi 1:7, 9
Malachi 3:8
Matthew 6:24
Matthew 19:23
Luke 12:16-20
Luke 12:21, 33

Honesty
Psalms 1:1-2
Psalms 37:37
Psalms 112:6
Proverbs 10:16
Proverbs 11:4
Proverbs 12:12
Proverbs 13:22
Proverbs 16:8, 11
Proverbs 19:1
Proverbs 21:3
Proverbs 22:1
Proverbs 28:6, 13
Matthew 7:20
Matthew 17:24
Luke 3:12-13
Luke 3:14
Luke 8:15
Luke 12:58
Luke 20:22-25
Romans 13:7
Romans 13:9
Galatians 6:9

Humility
Proverbs 22:4
Ecclesiastes 6:7-8
Jeremiah 9:24
Matthew 6:1-3
Luke 17:3
Luke 19:8
1 Corinthians 1:26
1 Corinthians 1:31

Industry
Proverbs 6:4
Proverbs 12:11
Proverbs 12:24
Proverbs 13:11
Proverbs 14:4
Proverbs 21:5
Proverbs 24:3-4
Matthew 20:13
Romans 12:11
1 Thessalonians 4:11

Inheritance
Proverbs 13:22

Proverbs 17:2
Proverbs 20:21
Ecclesiastes 2:18, 19
Ezekiel 46:16-18
Luke 15:11-31

Investments

Proverbs 21:20
Proverbs 24:27
Ecclesiastes 6:3
Matthew 6:19-21
Matthew 13:22
Matthew 24:35
Matthew 25:14-30
Matthew 25:45
Luke 14:28-29
Luke 19:13-26
2 Timothy 2:4
2 Peter 2:20
2 Peter 3:10

Laziness

Proverbs 6:6-11
Proverbs 12:24
Proverbs 13:11
Proverbs 14:4
Proverbs 21:17
2 Thessalonians 3:6
2 Thessalonians 3:10

Needs

Psalms 37:25
Matthew 6:8
Matthew 6:25-33
Philippians 4:19

Prosperity

Genesis 39:3
Deuteronomy 28:11
Deuteronomy 29:9
2 Chronicles 31:21
Psalms 1:3
Psalms 35:27
Proverbs 10:22
Proverbs 28:13
Jeremiah 17:8-10
Luke 6:38
John 10:10
2 Corinthians 8:9
Philippians 4:19
3 John 2

Prudence

Psalms 112:5
Proverbs 8:12
Proverbs 12:16, 23
Proverbs 13:16
Proverbs 14:8, 15, 18
Proverbs 15:5
Proverbs 16:21
Proverbs 18:15
Proverbs 22:3
Proverbs 27:12
Hosea 14:9
Amos 5:13

Saving

Proverbs 6:6-8
Proverbs 21:20
Proverbs 30:24, 25

Slothfulness

Proverbs 18:9
Proverbs 24:30, 31
Ecclesiastes 10:18
2 Thessalonians 3:11
Hebrews 6:12

Speculation

Ecclesiastes 5:15-17

Tithing and Giving
- Deuteronomy 14:22
- Deuteronomy 14:28
- Psalms 96:7-8
- Proverbs 3:9-10
- Proverbs 11:24-26
- Malachi 3:10
- Matthew 23:23
- Luke 6:38
- Luke 9:48
- Luke 21:1-4
- 1 Corinthians 9:9
- 1 Corinthians 9:10-11
- 1 Corinthians 9:14
- 1 Corinthians 16:1, 2
- 2 Corinthians 8:7-8
- 2 Corinthians 8:11-12
- 2 Corinthians 8:13-14
- 2 Corinthians 8:15
- 2 Corinthians 9:6-10
- Hebrews 7:1-2

Waste
- Genesis 41:36
- Luke 15:13
- John 6:12

Wealth
- Deuteronomy 8
- Psalms 60:10-12
- Proverbs 10:22
- Ecclesiastes 2:26
- Luke 12:16-21

SECTION 2

Home Budget

The key to financial success is to tell your money where to go, not try to figure out where it went. The only way to do this is to establish a realistic budget. The following pages contain a budget and record-keeping system that will enable you to gain financial freedom. The only way to do this is to *start today*.

Make it a family affair. Sit down with all members of the family and discuss family priorities. We cannot begin too early to impress our children with the importance of adequate planning for financial freedom. Let all members express their priorities and try to include them in your budget. The first go-around, don't leave anything out; this will be your ideal budget. If you are like most families (see Example), you will find yourself many dollars short of being able to meet this budget. Don't despair! Now is the time for the whole family to work together toward freedom. It is good for the children to learn that all things can't be obtained on whim, but that long-range planning is needed to reach many goals.

Make sure that every family member has something in the budget that he is going to benefit from: a trip to Disneyland, a new dress, a hunting trip, or even a horse! I included this example because it probably is one that comes up in many households and is probably considered by most adults (myself included) as somewhat foolish. God, however, wants to give us the desires of our heart. If one of your children wants this included in the budget (or some similar "foolish" expense), ask that child to pray about it. If, after seeking the Lord, he still wants it, put that expenditure in the budget. Say, "OK, we will begin by putting $4 a month aside for that expenditure. At that rate, it will probably take forever, but I'll make this bargain with you, as the Lord brings in extra money to the family, or as you earn extra money, we will put a share of it away in that fund for you." This now gives that child a part in the family plan and helps to justify some of the sacrifice that will be needed as your family moves toward freedom. (You might help the child look for a creative alternative to his dream. One young girl in our church used some of the money she was saving for a horse to put an ad in the local paper making herself available to work with and care for horses. She received an answer and is paid enough each month caring for the horse to cover all her bus fares to the place where the horse is kept and spending money too.)

Establish your goals. Prov. 16:3 tells us, "Commit thy works unto the Lord and thy thoughts will be established." It is important to establish goals to work toward. "Without a vision the people perish." This vision you have should be the written result of your family meeting.

This list of short-range and long-range goals should be someplace where all members of the family can view it from time to time. A word of caution here. These goals should not become the driving, binding forces of our life, sitting there to haunt and enslave us. Rather, our relationship with Jesus is our driving force and the goals a flexible and changeable plan for working within this relationship. If the budget or plan becomes the master, then we will be the slaves.

Make sure these goals are your goals. No one else can determine what is best for you and your family. Don't be forced into some "keep up with the Joneses" mold. You commit your work to God and let Him establish your ways.

Avoid credit. The biggest help to financial freedom will be to take every one of your credit cards and cut them into two pieces. Put one piece of the card under the sink in the bathroom and put the other one under the sink in the kitchen. This will avoid any possibility of divine healing. There is no way to back out of credit cards gradually; it must be done "cold turkey." Don't fool yourself by trying to put them in the top drawer of the dresser. Chapter 8 of *Your Money Matters* deals with this subject fully. Please read this chapter.

I cannot stress enough the terrible burden put on a family when the credit purchases begin to mount and the pressures of unpaid bills is heaped upon them. I know what you're saying, "We have control of our cards." If you had counselled as many families as I have, you would know the terrible trap that this attitude can be.

As a final warning, some of you are keeping your cards "just in case of an emergency." If this is your attitude, then you will have an emergency. A paraphrase of the end of Mark 11:23 is: "What you say is what you get." Perhaps you ought to rewrite Phil. 4:19, "But my God shall supply all my needs according to my VISA card."

Establish a budget. On the following pages is an actual case study showing you how to use the forms in this section.

Whom Do I Owe?

On this sheet, list everything that you owe other than the home mortgage. (If you have rental property, list the mortgages here and the income will be listed below.) Column five (percent of Total Due) is obtained by dividing the column one balance by the total of column one. In almost all budgets, by the time you list adequate living allowance, there is not enough remaining money to make the minimum contract payments due. Let us assume that the budget we eventually worked out only provided $150 for debt retirement. In that case I might approach the creditors in this example with the following plan:

Credit Union	$42	28%
Co-op	9	6%
BAC	21	18%
Finance Co.	78	48%
	$150	100%

(Note that this does not increase the payment to BAC to the full 27% ($40.50); rather it keeps this to the minimum and puts the extra payment to the finance company.)

At this point, some of you are doubtful whether this is going to work. Let me assure you, if you present a workable plan to your creditors, they will accept it. You will be pleasantly surprised to learn how willing your creditors are to work with you. When you show your plan to the creditors, oftentimes they can come up with helpful solutions.

What Are My Resources?

In this example, the husband is paid semi-monthly and the wife is not working. If you get paid weekly, budget for four paychecks per month. Four times a year you will have a "bonus" check that you can use for extras (if you get paid bi-weekly, you will have two "bonus" checks each year).

Other income can be things like rents, interests, baby-sitting, etc. Make sure you list everything.

WHOM DO I OWE?

NAME	1 BALANCE	2 DUE DATE	3 INTEREST PERCENT	4 CONTRACT MONTHLY PAYMENT	5 PERCENT OF TOTAL DUE	6 NEW BUDGET PAYMENT
Credit Union	450 00	5th	12%	45 00	28%	
Co-op	96 00	5th	12%	30 00	6%	
BAC	428 00	10th	18%	21 00	27%	
Finance Co.	629 00	7th	21%	157 25	39%	
TOTALS	1603 00			253 25		

WHAT ARE MY RESOURCES?

	PAY 1	PAY 2	PAY 3	PAY 4
Gross Salary	685 00	685 00		
Federal W/H	⟨81 80⟩	⟨81 80⟩		
FICA	⟨42 00⟩	⟨42 00⟩		
State W/H	⟨34 00⟩	⟨34 00⟩		
Work Comp.				
Health Insurance	⟨45 00⟩			
Life Insurance	⟨5 00⟩			
Union Dues	⟨9 00⟩			
Retirement				
Other —				
—				
Net Pay	468 20	527 20		
Other Income				
Child support		120 00		
—				
—				
FUNDS AVAILABLE	468 20	647 20		

Budget

On this form, first list your ideal budget. This budget would normally provide for savings and a reasonable allowance for clothes, vacations, gifts and the other "budget busters."

What you see here in this example is a very typical budget. The total expenses come to $1,778.25, while the net income available is only $1,115.40, or a shortage of $662.85. At this point, if this looks like your budget, *don't despair.*

Ours is a great God who can snatch victory from the jaws of defeat. Let's begin to see what can be done either to expand the income available or decrease expenses or both.

As you review this list of expenses you will note many differences from your own list (for example, a very *low* electric at only $37.00). Don't succumb to the temptation to stop because of your differences. Continue working with the figures until *your* budget is balanced!!

Explanation of additional items

Line 1—Savings—Once a budget has been balanced and debts paid off, you will likely have extra money to save and invest. It is the second level of savings and represents true savings since there is no plan to spend it. (Savings I is the money set aside for car repairs, Christmas, clothing, etc., and is really planned spending, not savings.)

Line 35—Debt Reduction—This is the total of your total monthly payments from the prior page, WHOM DO I OWE?

Line 38—Income Available—This is the total on line 40 from the prior page, WHAT ARE MY RESOURCES?

Line 39—Other—In balancing a budget, you will sometimes have a short-term income that is used to bring the budget into balance. That income is shown here, rather than line 38 (it could be gifts from parents, sale of assets, or drawings from savings).

BUDGET

#	ITEM	1 IDEAL BUDGET (Monthly)	2 INTERIM BUDGET (Monthly)	3 CASH or CHECK per Pay Period	4 TO SAVINGS per Pay Period	#
1	Savings II (Investments, etc.)					1
2	Tithe	149 00				2
3	Mortgage or Rent	448 00				3
4	Heat	30 00				4
5	Electricity	37 00				5
6	Water/Sewer	6 00				6
7	Garbage	4 75				7
8	Telephone	28 00				8
9	Car Insurance	28 25				9
10	Gasoline	100 00				10
11	Car Repairs	45 00				11
12	Recreation/Entertainment	10 00				12
13	Newspapers/Magazines	—				13
14	Health Insurance from check					14
15	Life Insurance	19 00				15
16	Doctors/Medical Expense	10 00				16
17	Food	195 00				17
18	Household	25 00				18
19	Cleaning/Dry Cleaning	—				19
20	Clothes	25 00				20
21	Home Furnishings	20 00				21
22	Contingencies	20 00				22
23	Christmas & Gifts	45 00				23
24	Vacation	35 00				24
25	Allowances	15 00				25
26	House Cleaning	25 00				26
27	Union Dues from check					27
28	Education	15 00				28
29	Child support	60 00				29
30	Day Care Center	130 00				30
31						31
32						32
33						33
34						34
35	Debt Reduction (from Whom Do I Owe?)	253 25				35
36						36
37	Total Expenses	1778 25				37
38	Net Income Available	1115 40				38
39	Other					39
40	Over/Short	(662 85)				40

Whom Do I Owe?

Rather than limit the payment to the finance company in this couple's case, we decided to limit the payment to the other creditors to interest only, to allow the payment of the last four installments to the finance company. Phone calls to the other three creditors were made and agreement was made to receive interest only for up to six months to allow this couple to put their plan to work. This will not hurt their credit standing! The company has reached a new agreement with you and, as long as you pay according to the new agreement, will give you a clear credit rating (to get this interest-only payment, you will have to surrender your credit cards). Note, we have reduced expenses by $81.50 per month.

What Are My Resources?

Most Americans over-withhold their taxes every year. While this generates large refunds come April, I have noted that most couples use the refund to pay off the charge purchases that have been accumulating during the year. This is a sign to me that the money is needed every month to meet bills. In this example, the couple has three children (all of whom are dependents), the wife is not working, and the husband has only one job. Question: How many exemptions is the husband allowed to claim?

Most of you will have replied five. The correct answer, as of June, 1980, is six. The tax tables are built heavy, to over-withhold on purpose. If you meet special criterion, you are entitled to a special withholding allowance for the purpose of figuring your withholding tax (it cannot be claimed when you file your tax return). Additional allowances can be claimed for itemized deductions you know you will have.

All of this information can be obtained by looking at the W-4 form you fill out to tell your employer how much tax to withhold.

In this example, we are able to increase the exemptions from three to eight, and increase the monthly net available from $966.40 to $1,080.00. An increase of $113.60 per month!

WHOM DO I OWE?

NAME	1 BALANCE	2 DUE DATE	3 INTEREST PERCENT	4 CONTRACT MONTHLY PAYMENT	5 PERCENT of TOTALDUE	6 NEW BUDGET PAYMENT
Credit Union	450 00	5th	12%	45 00	28%	4 50
Co-op	96 00	5th	12%	30 00	6%	2 50
BAC	428 00	10th	18%	21 00	27%	7 50
Finance Company	629 00	7th	21%	157 25	39%	157 25
TOTALS	1603 00			253 25		171 75

WHAT ARE MY RESOURCES?

	PAY 1	PAY 2	PAY 3	PAY 4	After Exemption Change	
Gross Salary	685 00	685 00			685 00	685 00
Federal W/H	(81 80)	(81 80)			(41 00)	(41 00)
FICA	(42 00)	(42 00)			(42 00)	(42 00)
State W/H	(34 00)	(34 00)			(18 00)	(18 00)
Work Comp.						
Health Insurance	(45 00)				(45 00)	
Life Insurance	(5 00)				(5 00)	
Union Dues	(9 00)				(9 00)	
Retirement						
Other —						
—						
Net Pay	468 20	527 20			525 00	584 00
Other Income						
Child support		120 00				120 00
—						
—						
FUNDS AVAILABLE	468 20	647 20			525 00	704 00

Budget

Now we go to the interim budget column. In this column we list the budget that we will be on until the debts are paid in full, raises received and our goal of a balanced ideal budget is reached. In the budget section are several blank forms so that you can revise this interim budget during the year. The section on practical applications shares many hints on how to reduce your expenses.

One thing that helped this budget was the sale of an unused pickup sitting in their backyard. As you work toward financial freedom, be sensitive to selling nonused and highly depreciating items. Have a garage sale to get going.

Column three shows what will be set aside each pay period to meet the budgeted expenses. Those with a C by them are taken in cash, and the remainder left in the checking account to write the check when the bill is due.

Column four is the record of the money transferred to the savings account each pay period to assure that money will be available when the bill is due. These are expenses that are not paid every month, but we know that they will come due. This is very similar to an envelope system used by many couples. As each pay check is cashed, certain amounts are put into labeled envelopes to assure that cash is available when the bill is due. Rather than leave this around in cash, we're putting it into the bank.

The best way to do this is to have a fixed amount taken from your check each pay period and put into the credit union. If you don't have a credit union, have your bank automatically transfer the money from your checking account to a savings account. In other words, don't trust yourself to do it!

The amounts being set aside for clothes, car repairs, vacation, etc., are probably not enough, but it is better to have something than nothing. Set *something* aside, even if it is only a few dollars a month. Begin to prepare to live your life on a cash basis.

Even after we've pared this budget to the bare minimums, there is still an anticipated shortage of $63.75 per month. This shortage will have to be made up for the next four months (until the finance company is paid) by part-time work, direct sales, garage sales or additional expense savings. The nice thing about this budget process is that we know how much we have to trust God for each month.

BUDGET

	ITEM	1 IDEAL BUDGET (Monthly)	2 INTERIM BUDGET (Monthly)	3 CASH or CHECK per Pay Period	4 TO SAVINGS per Pay Period
1	Savings 2 (Investments, etc.)				
2	Tithe	149.00	149.00	74.50	
3	Mortgage or Rent	448.00	448.00	224.00	
4	Heat	30.00	20.00	10.00	
5	Electricity	37.00	27.00	13.50	
6	Water/Sewer	6.00	6.00	3.00	
7	Garbage	4.75	4.75	2.37	
8	Telephone	28.00	20.00	10.00	
9	Car Insurance	28.25	28.25		14.13
10	Gasoline	100.00	80.00 c	40.00	
11	Car Repairs	45.00	15.00		7.50
12	Recreation/Entertainment	10.00	10.00	5.00	
13	Newspapers/Magazines	—	—		
14	Health Insurance *from check*				
15	Life Insurance	19.00	19.00	9.50	
16	Doctors/Medical Expense	10.00	10.00		5.00
17	Food	195.00	160.00 c	80.00	
18	Household	25.00	20.00 c	10.00	
19	Cleaning/Dry Cleaning	—			
20	Clothes	25.00	12.00		6.00
21	Home Furnishings	20.00	8.00		4.00
22	Contingencies	20.00	8.00		4.00
23	Christmas & Gifts	45.00	13.00		6.50
24	Vacation	35.00	12.00		6.00
25	Allowances	15.00	7.00 c	3.50	
26	House Cleaning	25.00			
27	Union Dues *from check*				
28	Education	15.00	6.00		3.00
29	*Child support*	60.00	60.00	30.00	
30	*Day Care Center*	130.00	28.00	14.00	
31					
32					
33					
34					
35	Debt Reduction (from Whom Do I Owe?)	253.25	171.75	85.88	
36					
37	Total Expenses	1778.25	1342.75	615.25	56.13
38	Net Income Available	1115.40	1229.00		
39	Other (*Truck Sale 4 Mos.*)		50.00		
40	Over/Short	⟨662.85⟩	⟨63.75⟩		

Budget amounts:

Car repairs	—	15.5¢ per mile for maintenance and new purchase
Doctors/Medical	—	$100 per year per person
Clothing	—	$100 per year per person
Furniture	—	$150 per year, plus actual planned expenditures
Contingencies	—	$10 minimum per month for unplanned expenses
Gifts	—	the average family spends $300 on Christmas alone—this is not needed, but is normally done.
Vacation	—	actual cost of where you plan to go. A driving/camping vacation will cost about $30 per day for a family of 4.

Budget Percentages:

25-40	Housing
20-35	Food
7-13	Car
7	Consumer Debt
6-10	Insurance
6-9	Entertainment
5-7	Clothes
5-10	Medical
3-10	Savings
3-4	Gifts/Christmas
2-3	Wife Support
2-4	Allowances
2-8	Furniture
2-5	Education
5%	Contingencies
100-170%	

Budget Payment Per Pay Period

Just forecasting a balanced budget will not always do the job. After balancing your cash flow, you need to examine where you are. This form allows you to plan exactly which bills are going to be paid each pay period.

When we did this with our case couple, we discovered a real problem; we were $471.11 short in the first two paychecks! Again, this is typical, so don't despair.

At this time, you need to re-examine the expenditures to see which you can revise or put off on a short-term basis.

Note for Balanced Budgets

Some of you may be fortunate enough not to be in debt and have a balanced budget and no past due accounts. If this is the case, you can skip this form if you like. Actually, this is the form that I use more than others because it allows me to accurately forecast cash flow shortages in advance. The decision is yours.

Line 38—From Savings—In our planned budget, we are transferring money into Savings I to pay for car insurance, clothes, etc. When these expenses actually come due, we transfer the money back out of savings into the checking account. It may seem to be a hassle to be putting the money in and out in the same month, but I've learned the importance of keeping those funds out of my checkbook balance until they are actually needed.

BUDGETED PAYMENT PER PAY PERIOD

		1	2	3	4	5	6
		Period 1 12/18	Period 2 1/3	Period 3 1/18	Period 4 2/3	Period 5 2/18	Period 6 3/3
1	CASH:						
2	Car Gas	40 00	40 00	40 00	40 00		
3	Allowances/Cleaning	3 50	3 50	3 50	3 50		
4	Food/Household	90 00	90 00	90 00	90 00		
5	Entertainment	5 00	5 00	5 00	5 00		
6							
7	REGULAR CHECKS:						
8	Mort./Rent		448 00		448 00		
9	Heat	24 20		25 00			
10	Electricity		27 00		27 00		
11	Water/Sewer		6 40		6 00		
12	Garbage	4 75		4 75			
13	Telephone	28 25		20 00			
14	Newspapers						
15	Tithe	30 50	68 50	80 50	68 50		
16	Medical Ins.						
17	Union Dues						
18	To Savings (1)	56 13	56 13	56 13	56 13		
19	To Savings (2)						
20	Debt Payments		171 75		171 75		
21	Life Insurance	19 00		19 00			
22	Child support	60 00	60 00		60 00		
23	Day Care	65 00	28 00		28 00		
24							
25	Car Insurance		169 50				
26	Magazines						
27	Life Insurance						
28	Car Repairs						
29	Medical						
30	Clothes						
31	Furniture						
32	Gifts	50 00					
33	Vacation						
34	Contingencies						
35	Education						
36	Total Expenses	526 33	1173 78	343 88	1003 88		
37	Net Income Available	704 00	525 00	704 00	525 00		
38	From Savings						
39	Other — Truck			50 00			
40	Over/Short	177 67	⟨648 78⟩	910 12	⟨478 88⟩		

Budgeted Per Pay Period

For the first two paychecks, we reduced the car gas and grocery expense by $5 each. This is short term only and means that care will have to be taken to keep in the budget. Note that these are taken in cash. When the cash runs out, don't spend anymore! Look to the Lord to provide.

We cut down the amount going to savings the first two checks (Savings I is the amount set aside in our "envelope" system—Savings II is for investments, etc.) and changed the transfer to savings to once a month to correspond with the mid-month check. This makes more sense with this couple because of the extra withholdings at the first of the month.

The life insurance was whole life, so we arranged to pay the premium with the cash value for two months. This reduces the amount of insurance in the event of death, so make sure it gets paid back eventually.

Debt payments were reduced by making arrangements with the finance company to skip a payment. Most finance companies have this "skip payment" plan. It is expensive interest, but it allows us to get the plan into gear.

The auto insurance company was contacted and arrangements made to pay the premium late. No loss of coverage was incurred, but did allow us to coordinate our savings transfer and car insurance payment (see savings record).

Finally, a re-examination of needs for Christmas showed that $10, not $50, was needed.

Note that the money for the gifts, and later the insurance, was transferred into the checking account from savings. What we are doing here is taking the money out of the "envelope" and spending it.

The totals for the three pay periods:

12/18	over	$309.50
1/3	short	(265.23)
1/18	over	$309.50
		$353.77

We have a surplus of $353.77 to meet the anticipated 2/3 deficit of $422.75. At this point, we don't know where the $68.98 will come from, but we have more than 6 weeks to work with before this deficit need be met. Once this deficit is met, we will be faced with the budgeted deficit of $63.75 on 3/3.

BUDGETED PAYMENT PER PAY PERIOD

#		Period 1 12/18	Period 2 1/3	Period 3 1/18	Period 4 2/3	Period 5 2/18	Period 6 3/3
1	CASH:						
2	Car Gas	35.00	35.00	40.00	40.00	40.00	40.00
3	Allowances/Cleaning	3.50	3.50	3.50	3.50	3.50	3.50
4	Food/Household	85.00	85.00	90.00	90.00	90.00	90.00
5	Entertainment	5.00	5.00	5.00	5.00	5.00	5.00
6							
7	REGULAR CHECKS:						
8	Mort./Rent		448.00		448.00		448.00
9	Heat	24.20		20.00		20.00	
10	Electricity		27.00		27.00		27.00
11	Water/Sewer		6.40		6.00		6.00
12	Garbage	4.75		4.75		4.75	
13	Telephone	28.25		20.00		20.00	
14	Newspapers						
15	Tithe	80.50	68.50	80.50	68.50	80.50	68.50
16	Medical Ins.						
17	Union Dues						
18	To Savings (1)	18.80	37.33	112.25		112.25	
19	To Savings (2)						
20	Debt Payments	14.50	14.50		171.75		171.75
21	Life Insurance	—		—		19.00	
22	Child support	30.00	60.00	30.00	60.00		60.00
23	Day Care	65.00			28.00		28.00
24							
25	Car Insurance			169.50			
26	Magazines						
27	Life Insurance						
28	Car Repairs						
29	Medical						
30	Clothes						
31	Furniture						
32	Gifts	10.00					
33	Vacation						
34	Contingencies						
35	Education						
36	Total Expenses	404.50	790.23	575.50	947.75	395.00	947.75
37	Net Income Available	704.00	525.00	704.03	525.00	704.00	525.00
38	From Savings	10.00		131.00			
39	Other — Truck			50.00		50.00	
40	Over/Short	309.50	⟨265.23⟩	309.50	⟨422.75⟩	359.00	⟨422.75⟩

Spending Summary

This summary allows you to keep track of the balances in each account. Group them as follows:

Cash:	*Checking:*	*Savings:*
Car gas	Mortgage	Car Insurance
Cleaning	Heat	Life Insurance
Food	Electricity	Car Repairs
Household	Water/Sewer	Medical
Entertainment	Garbage	Clothes
	Telephone	Furniture
	Newspapers/ magazines	Gifts
		Vacation
	Medical Insurance	Education
	Union Dues	Contingencies
	Debt Payments	

As you deposit your check in the account, divide the deposit between the various accounts and note all checks drawn and cash spent on these forms. If everything balances (rarely will it come to the exact balance because we often forget to write things down—but we should be fairly close) the total cash we have should equal the balances in the cash account and the balance in our checkbook should equal the balances of the checking group.

The spending record is for you to keep track of all your expenses. This is an absolute must for the first three months of your budget! I know it is a pain, and you'd rather pull weeds, wash the car, *anything* other than become a bookkeeper! There are two reasons you must keep track of your expenses.

First, the vast majority of you have no idea where you spend your money. With most budgets, it is not the large expenses that upset the plan; it is the little $1.00 to $5.00 that seem to sift through your fingers. How can you adequately budget for clothes for the coming year if you don't know how much you spent last year? Record keeping is needed to control these expenses.

Second, since you will be keeping track of every expense (keep a little memo book in your pocket or purse to record these expenses), there will be times when you are about to reach for

HOUSEHOLD
ACCOUNT

$20.00
BUDGET

DATE		TRANSACTION	ALLOCATED	SPENT	BALANCE
		Balance from November			34 02
12	3	Allocation from paycheck	10 00		44 02
12	18	Allocation from paycheck	10 00		54 02
12	20	Cash at Safeway-household		4 95	49 07
12	24	Check #572 - Amway for cleaning supplies		24 40	24 67
1	3	Allocation from paycheck	10 00		34 67

FOOD
ACCOUNT

$75.00
BUDGET

DATE		TRANSACTION	ALLOCATED	SPENT	BALANCE
		Balance Forward			12 03
12	18	Allocation from paycheck	75 00		87 03
12	18	Check #566 - Safeway		37 83	49 20
12	20	Cash - Albertsons		9 27	39 93
12	23	Cash - Safeway		4 93	35 00
12	28	Cash - ABC Discount Foods		32 50	2 50
1	3	Allocation from paycheck	75 00		77 50

fifty cents to buy something and say to yourself, "If I buy this I'm going to have to write it down and show it to my wife/husband when we get home tonight." So you won't buy it! That's great! Now you're beginning to change your buying habits and that's exactly what most of us need to do.

This form is also used to keep track of the "envelope" balances. By keeping track of these expenses in this manner, we always know how much we have available to meet expenses.

In our example, we transferred in only $18.80, broken between car insurance ($8.80) and gifts ($10.00). We immediately withdrew the $10.00 we had budgeted for gifts and put it back into the checking account to cover a check written to Penneys.

On January 3, a check transferred $37.33 to savings. For the sake of this illustration, we showed it as all being reserved for car insurance.

Starting with January 18, the bank will automatically transfer $112.25 from the checking account to the savings account. Our entry then shows how much goes into each "envelope."

On the 2nd, we transfer out $131.00 to help cover the car insurance premium of $169.50. Normally, this amount would be exactly what was due. Remember, in the illustration we were looking for short-term ways to cut expenses.

I think you begin to see why this savings system is set up. Even though you only have $74.38 available for the car insurance premium, the fact that you have been setting money aside for all of these expenses allows you to create your own "loan fund" and borrow from yourself. The total of all the savings balances was $158.38.

As your income expands and debts are paid off, increase the amounts transferred to savings. It may take a few years, but you'll eventually have the money to meet these expenses before they arise.

If on February 21, you need $14.00 worth of work done on the car, what will you do? You have $30.00 in your car repair fund. Praise the Lord, the expense is covered.

The one danger point with this system is not to get to the point where you are depending on your system instead of the Lord. Remember that God is your supplier, not the savings account!

SPENDING SUMMARY

ACCOUNT: Gifts **BUDGET:** $13.00

DATE		TRANSACTION	1	ALLOCATED	SPENT	BALANCE
12	18			10.00		10.00
12	19	Christmas			10.00	⊖
1	18			13.00		13.00
2	18			13.00		26.00

ACCOUNT: Car Insurance **BUDGET:** $28.25

DATE		TRANSACTION	1	ALLOCATED	SPENT	BALANCE
12	18			8.80		8.80
1	3			37.33		46.13
1	18			28.25		74.38
2	2				131.00	⟨56.62⟩
2	18			28.25		⟨28.37⟩

ACCOUNT: Car Repairs **BUDGET:** $15.00

DATE		TRANSACTION	1	ALLOCATED	SPENT	BALANCE
1	18			15.00		15.00
2	18			15.00		30.00

A Final Note

As you look at this, you're probably saying, "I'll never be able to do this. I'm not a CPA." All I ask is that you commit yourself to trying to do this for three months.

Remember the first day you started the job you're now on? Remember how, at the end of the day's instructions, you said to yourself, "I'll never be able to do this"? Now, after applying yourself to that task, it has become second nature—you are used to the various tasks.

After working with this budget for three months, you will be able to teach others. I think you'll find that the system provides you freedom, not bondage.

If you run into any problems, drop me a note and I'll respond as quickly as possible! Malcolm D. MacGregor, Your Money Matters, P.O. Box 82, Gresham, Oregon 97030.

SECTION 3

Seminar Study Guide

The following section can be used as a self-study guide in financial freedom. You might find it beneficial to get a set of seminar tapes from your local bookstore. The tapes are entitled, "Your Money Matters." You may order these directly from the publisher: Dimension Tapes, 6820 Auto Club Road, Minneapolis, Minnesota 55438, your Successful Living Dealer, or me.

The format of this section is designed to leave you room in each section to write notes and put some of your own thoughts down. As you make commitments to the Lord in areas of correction, put them in red with the date by them. A review of this book later can remind you of this commitment.

Finances—God's Barometer

1. *DEVELOP OUR TRUSTWORTHINESS* (Luke 16:8-12; note verse 11). Just as parents need to be able to trust their children through nurture and discipline so God wants to build into us wisdom and God's grace.

2. *DEMONSTRATE GOD'S CARE FOR US* (Matt. 6:31-32; also, 6:8; Deut. 28:12-13). As God meets our every need, we demonstrate how much He cares for us.

3. *DEMONSTRATE HIS LOVE* (Matt. 7:11).

4. *DEMONSTRATE HIS POWER* (2 Chron. 16:9). Psalm 1 seems to guarantee success if we will:

(a) Obtain advice from Christian brothers and sisters;
(b) Have the right group of friends;
(c) Be positive thinkers;
(d) Meditate on His Word.

5. *UNIFY CHRISTIANS* (1 Tim. 5:8). Paul charges the care of one's family to the church body. We are dependent upon one another (see 2 Cor. 8:14, 15). Satan's most effective weapon is breaking Christians' dependence upon each other.

6. *DEMONSTRATE OUR COMMITMENT TO OTHERS* (Deut. 15:11). This is done especially in reaching out to the poor.

7. *DECLARE HIS DIRECTION* (Prov. 3:6; Ps. 65:11; 37:25).

(a) *True needs vs. wants* (Luke 11:11, 12; Phil. 4:19)

(b) *Testing Faith* (*Ask* plus *Believe=Receive*)

"Don't trust facts, trust Truth." That is accomplished by building faith gradually.

(c) *Misspent Finances* (Prov. 21:20)

(d) *Violated Principles*

1. Poverty attitude (Prov. 10:15)
2. Stinginess (Prov. 11:24)
3. Stubbornness (Prov. 13:18)
4. Laziness (Prov. 6:11, 20:13)
5. Gluttony/Drunkenness (Prov. 23:21)
6. Craftiness (Prov. 28:19, 20)
7. Hastiness (Prov. 28:22)

(e) *Major Change in Direction*

1. Method
2. Scope
3. Location
4. Vocation

Money Mistakes

SOLUTIONS		CHALLENGES
Rom. 13:8	(1) Debt-Oriented Life	Prov. 22:7
1 Tim. 6:8	(2) Bill-Oriented Life Prov. 30:7-9	Matt. 6:24-34
1 Cor. 10:31	(3) Money-Oriented Life	1 Tim. 6:9

Matt. 6:19	(4) Investment-Oriented Life	Matt. 13:22
Matt. 6:33	(5) Business-Oriented Life 1. God—Ps. 127:1 2. Family—Gen. 2:24 3. Ministry—Matt. 19:21 4. Work—Ps. 127:2	2 Tim. 2:4
Prov. 2:11	(6) "Get-Rich-Quick"	Prov. 28:22
Acts 24:16	(7) Financial Guilt-Oriented	Prov. 15:16

God's Tree of Financial Freedom

1. *GIVING*—Roots (Luke 6:38: If you give you will get.)
   (a) *Give to God*—Mal. 3:10; Prov. 3:9, 10
   (b) *Give to Family*—1 Tim. 5:8
   (c) *Give to the Poor*—Luke 3:11; Matt. 5:42; Prov. 14:21, 31
   (d) *Give to Christian Work*—1 Cor. 9:7; 9:14
   (e) *Give to Other Christians*—1 John 3:17; James 3:15

2. *RECEIVING*—Trunk (Mal. 3:10; Luke 6:38)
   (a) *Hard Labor*—Prov. 10:4; 13:4
   (b) *God's Provision*—Prov. 31:10-31
   (c) *Answered Prayer*—Heb. 11:6; Phil. 4:6

3. *SPENDING*—Branches
   (a) *Sales Resistance*—Prov. 20:14
   (b) *Look for the Best Buys*—Prov. 31:18
   (c) *Promptness in Paying*—Prov. 3:28

Guidance to Avoid Impulse Buying

1. *DO WE REALLY NEED IT?*
2. Is the price reasonable? (Establish *your* price and hold.)
3. Is this the best time to buy?
4. If a bargain, is it the current model?
5. If on sale, is it true sale price? (Note difference between asking price and sale price—at least 10% variance.)
6. Is there no item that can serve as a substitute? (Pay cash!) (Buy used?)
7. Are there no major disadvantages?
8. Although excessive price, will it satisfy an inner need?
9. Have I researched the item?
10. Do I know the retailer's reputation?
11. Does retailer offer special services?

If you answer to the above:

9-11	Yes	BUY
6-8	Yes	THINK
0-5	Yes	DON'T BUY

Why Not Credit Buying?

1. Too easy to buy nonessentials.
2. Don't need credit cards to establish credit.
3. Satan's alternative is CREDIT CARDS, based on mistrust.
4. Spend more on credit than buy on sale.
5. Possible to get cash discount; use discount stores.

Best Shopping Formula

1. *AVOID CREDIT CARDS!*
2. Make list and *stick to it.* Use coupons.
3. Shop alone.
4. *Know your store.* Note layout designed to foster impulse buying and end-aisle fake "sales."
5. Try to be in and out in 30 minutes.
6. Shop for food the last week of the month—best sales always! (Save 20% of shopping money; buy in cases last week of month.)

7. Eat *before* shopping.
8. Don't touch items. You are always more likely to buy.
9. Agree upon the Lord to lead you to the best sales.
10. Check bottom shelf—also different labels on same product (e.g., tomatoes).
11. Don't buy sides of meat. Buy on sale in quantity.
12. Compare stores.
13. Have a budget and stick to it for food.
14. Note that chain markets have best comparisons on items.
15. Stock inventory of toiletries.
16. Understand unit pricing.
17. Get a pocket calculator.

The Myth of the Working Mother

1. *FINANCIAL PROBLEMS:* Woman with two children and working husband:

Wage: $ Gross: $

Expenses:
- Taxes
- Tithe
- Transportation
- Lunches
- Carry-out food
- Extra clothes
- Forfeited savings (prepared foods, shopping waste, extra clothes, etc.)
- Hairdresser, etc.
- "I owe it to myself"
- Employment Expense
- Baby-sitter
- Exp. of lost nurture ______

Total $ Week ($) deficit

Working mother needs to gross $ / month to break even.

2. *EMOTIONAL PROBLEMS* come to a woman who is also a mother, wife, as well as a provider. Further, there is the problem of the family (and husband) becoming dependent upon

the wife's income. Even more serious is the possibility of transferred affection due to working relationships.

Needs of the home should be provided by husband's salary. If the wife wants to work and the children are all in school, then part-time work is appropriate. The wife's salary should go directly into savings, rather than living on it or relying upon it.

3. *COTTAGE INDUSTRIES*
   (a) Make merchandise in home for gifts or sales.
   (b) Design clothes.
   (c) Make nutritional meals—planning, advice, save expenses.
   (d) Invest through restoration—resale items.
   (e) Wise buying.
   (f) Direct sales (Amway, Avon, Successful Living, Right Time Books, etc.)
   (g) Babysitting ministry.

Basics for Financial Freedom

1. *Acknowledge ownership* of money, time, possessions and earning power to be God's.
   (a) Possession is not ownership (Deut. 10:14; Ps. 24:1; Hag. 2:8).
   (b) What we have isn't obtained by ourselves (Deut. 8:17-18).
   (c) God doesn't have us until He has everything (Rom. 12:1).
2. *Make specific commitment* to gain financial freedom.
3. *Establish a clear ministry purpose in your life* (Prov. 30:7-9).
4. *Tithe*—Weekly reminder of our commitment to God. Christians will be locked into debt if they do not tithe.
5. *Plan for abundance* (Luke 12:22-36).
   (a) Have true estimate of life—"more than these" (v. 23).
   (b) God knows your needs (v. 30).
   (c) Seek Kingdom of God first (v. 31).
   (d) Fear not ("perfect love casts out all fear"); pray the Lord's protection about your family constantly—ministry of angels (v. 32).
   (e) Convert material goods to ministering currency (e.g., if

your home is the Lord's, you will desire hospitality, v. 33).
(f) Take stance of warrior (v. 35).
(g) Take stance of somebody ready to leave (v. 36).

6. *Plan for distribution of goods at your death* (1 Tim. 5:8; Luke 12:20).
7. *Get out of debt.*
   (a) Establish husband as one responsible for knowing budget and seeing all is paid. In husband-wife effort, the husband is ultimately responsible.
   (b) List all expenses—regular and incidental.
   (c) Have a friend review priorities listed.
   (d) Discern nonessentials.
   (e) Sell high-depreciating, unused items.
   (f) Begin on cash basis and prayer basis.
   (g) Avoid "get-rich-quick" pitches (Prov. 28:22).
8. *Evaluate each expense and how it will work for and benefit reputation of God* (1 Cor. 10:31; Ps. 23:3).
9. *Never put God in a financial corner by buying on "faith"* (Matt. 4:6, 7).
10. *Don't borrow for depreciating items.*
    (a) Violates Scripture's highest potential (Rom. 13:8).
    (b) Bondage to man (Prov. 22:7).
    (c) Pressures the future (James 4:13). Set aside funds for future to purchase depreciating items such as cars, versus borrowing on credit.
    (d) Pressure of insecurity (1 Tim. 5:8).
    (e) Limits God (2 Cor. 9:11). Be sensitive to utilize surpluses available in the body; do not incur consumer debt.
    (f) Harmful (Isa. 55:8, 9).
    (g) Harms God's reputation (Phil. 4:19).
11. *Do not loan for nonessentials.* Be sensitive to the poor and thus lend to God (Prov. 19:17).
12. *Never co-sign.* This brings people into master-servant bondage and destroys Christian relationships (Prov. 6:1; 11:15; 17:18; 20:16; 22:26; 27:13).
13. *Develop sales resistance* (Prov. 20:14).
    (a) Note: Make claims you need least (e.g., "Salem's like a breath of fresh air"; are generally untrue).
    (b) What will you do with it once you have it?

(c) Is it more than you need?
(d) Is there unnecessary overhead?

Having made decisions in faith and with counsel, stand by it and await God's provision, lest you faint *and* become double minded.

14. *Develop skills in simple maintenance.*
15. *Determine God's reason for lack of funds.*
    (a) Do not need. (b) Test faith. (c) Misspent. (d) Violates scripture. (e) Major change coming. Don't reduce your relationship with God to a formula.
16. *Discern needs and pray for wants* (1 Tim. 6:6-10).
17. *Prepare for financial breathing* (Phil. 4:11-12).
18. *Be sensitive to God's direction in giving:*
    (a) Is church communicating messages through Scripture?
    (b) Is there positive response from the people?
    (c) Does leadership illustrate the message?
    (d) Is church reproducing spiritually? (Not necessarily numbers.)
    (e) Is there standard of excellence with minimum of expense?

Tithing

Ten percent of increase is not take-home pay! *Gen. 14:16-20* lays a foundation for bringing tithes, which are paid to God, into the storehouse. Principles of tithing precedes the laws; expression of covenant relationship and trust; love commitment based upon grace. Gifts and offerings are beyond the tithe.

Giving

Giving comes after the tithe: tithe is not giving. It is *paid.*

The foundations are: God is our supplier (Phil. 4:19); give in order to place yourself in position to receive; must expect betterment by God's grace (Matt. 13:3; Mark 11:23).

Injunctions (2 Cor. 9:7) are: Give willingly from the heart; must not give grudgingly; must not give out of compulsion; must be done cheerfully.

Saving

If you are not managing money, money is managing you. You need vision.

Savings for sake of savings not good because:

- Lose sight of God (Deut. 8:13).
- Creates greed (Ps. 62:10).
- Endangers integrity (Prov. 28:20).
- Results in barrenness of life (Mark 4:19).
- Hinders entrance to Kingdom of God (Matt. 19:23).
- Subjects people to powerful temptations (1 Tim. 6:9).

Percent Net Income

7% car payment

25-40%	Housing (including utilities)
20-35%	Food/Household 200-600
~~7-13%~~	Car (not car payment)
7%	Consumer debt
6-10%	Insurance
6- 9%	Entertainment/Recreation/Vacation
5- 7%	Clothes
5-10%	Medical/Dental
3-10%	Savings (10% good)
3- 4%	Gifts/Christmas
2- 3%	"Wife Support"
2- 4%	Allowances
2- 8%	Furniture
2- 5%	Education
5%	Contingencies
100-170%	

Budget Formula on working income (after tithe and taxes):

- 10% Savings/Investment
- 75% Living Expenses
- 15% Debt Clearance and Buffer

(Absolute maximum, but better to get down to the 7% in formula above).

Closing Tips

Begin to build savings for retirement only about 15 years before retirement age. Get debts into manageable position, especially by creating your own loan fund on regular basis through savings. This avoids debt pyramid, thereby increasing living allowance. Get away from bondage to checkbook by using cash as much as possible until you develop discipline with checks.

SECTION 4

Practical Applications

General

Make shopping less convenient; destroy your credit cards.

Don't over withhold on income taxes.

Calculate cost in hours worked. Perhaps you are about to buy a stereo for $480. If your wage is $5.00 per hour, this means 96 hours of work or almost 2½ weeks. Actually, to clear $480 after taxes, you will probably have to earn $600 or 3 solid weeks to buy the stereo. Makes you think twice, doesn't it?

Shop around for the best savings rate you can find. Many times your local credit union can be very competitive.

Put most of your effort into saving on big ticket items. A 10% savings on a car is going to be much more than a 10% savings on a can of peaches.

Don't confuse price with quality. Just because something costs more doesn't mean that it is better.

Shop around for the best rates on your checking account service.

Save on postage by using postcards for short notes.

Shop seasonally:

- January—post-holiday clearances and white sales.
- February—Washington and Lincoln birthday sales; big winter clearances.
- March—winter sports equipment are great this month.
- April—After Easter clothing sales and big canned goods sales.
- May—Memorial Day sales on garden and vacation items.
- June—Frozen food sales.
- July—4th of July sales and some summer clothes will start on sale.

August—Back-to-school sales; summer sports items on clearance.
September—Home improvement sales, pre-holiday sales and end of year-model cars.
October—Veteran's Day sales.
November and December—The worst months to buy anything; get Christmas shopping done by November 15.

Mortgage or rent

Decide on whether to rent or buy. If you know you're only going to be in the area for less than two years, renting may be cheapest.

With the high cost of homes, look to a mobile home as an alternative. The move in cost is quite low and, of late, they have been appreciating in value rather than depreciating. This could be an excellent way to start building some equity.

Two rules of thumb: (1) The house should cost between two and a half to three times your gross annual income. (2) The total house operating expenses, including mortgage, taxes, insurance and house operations, should not exceed 25% of monthly income. (At today's prices and costs, it is next to impossible to live within these parameters. Don't let the monthly cost exceed 40%.)

Check the community before you buy. Find an area that shows pride of ownership and select one of the least expensive homes in the area (your equity will grow faster).

A home four to ten years old will normally offer a modern floor plan and utilities and will avoid immediate costs of landscaping and drapes.

Older homes can be great buys, but they will usually cost more in maintenance and repairs.

Note the following questions:

1. Have a termite inspection.
2. Check exterior walls for sagging and interior walls for cracking.
3. Have an electrician check the adequacy of wiring.
4. Is the heating plant adequate?
5. Is it insulated? Make sure that at least the ceiling is insulated.
6. Plumbing—is it on sewer or septic? If septic, have it

checked by an expert. Also, check with planning to see if a sewer assessment is soon forthcoming.

7. Check the water for quality. Hard water and impurities can corrode plumbing.
8. Is the hot-water heater adequate? Check for rust or signs of leaks.
9. Check the roof and gutters. Check ceilings and walls for signs of water.
10. When was the last exterior paint job?

When moving in, remember, the down payment is not the only cash you need. Be sure to keep a reserve for repairs, minor remodeling, landscaping, drapes, moving costs, etc. The furniture that was so nice in the old home, oftentimes does not fit into the new home at all.

Make sure you save all receipts for the permanent improvements you make on your house; you'll need them for tax purposes some day.

Heat

Turn your thermostat down to 64°. This will make your house cool, but a sweater will remove the chill. Two things will happen. First, your family will experience fewer colds. Second, you will save up to 15% on your heating bill.

If yours is a 1,000-square-foot home and you don't have insulation in the ceiling, you can save from $100 to $600 a year by insulating.

Keep the damper on your fireplace closed. A tight-seal glass screen can more than pay for itself.

Check the rubber or felt weather stripping and replace it if you see signs of wear.

Sliding doors can cause much heat to be lost. In colder country, storm doors can pay for themselves in two years.

Tape or tack up plastic sheets over the windows.

Have your furnace checked and cleaned.

Put fan on manual—not automatic.

Add a wood-burning stove where wood is plentiful and cheap (we saved $400 in one year alone).

Use blankets, not heat, for night-time use.

Turn down heat if you are going to be gone for a couple of days.

Electricity

The most expensive appliance in your home is the hot-water heater. Keep it at 120°. Insulate the heater and all exposed hot-water pipes.

Turn off lights when you are not in the room. Use reduced wattage bulbs in areas where you won't be reading or where the light is for effect.

Buy 130-volt light bulbs (try not to go lower than 125). Those will last much longer than less expensive bulbs.

Stop the dishwasher before the drying cycle. Simply opening the washer a crack will allow the steam to dissipate, and the heat will normally dry the dishes (blot the tops of the glasses just after opening).

Telephone

Study your usage and decide whether you need a private line.

If you have relatively few outgoing calls, some areas have a reduced rate for those people who do not exceed certain outgoing levels.

Do you really need those fancy-style phones? Money can be saved using basic black. Many areas no longer charge for colors.

On long distance calls, can a letter do?

If you must call long distance, call at reduced-rate times. Generally the cheapest rate is after 11:00 p.m. and before 8:00 a.m., and all day Saturday and Sunday to 5:00 p.m.

Many states offer very cheap intra-state calls after certain times of the evening.

Other Utilities

A leaky faucet will use 6,000 gallons of water a year. The cost to replace a washer is about 4¢.

Leaking toilets can consume close to 1,000 gallons of water per month.

Making periodic trips to the local dump can be much less expensive than paying the extra cost to have extra trash picked up by your weekly service.

Because of recycling, some families can save cans and bottles, burn paper and compost the balance. Check your local laws, some areas make garbage service mandatory.

Car Expenses

One of the most obvious areas, and one very often overlooked, is the car manual. Study it and know the maintenance required for your car. Keep to this schedule.

Inflate tires 2-4 pounds above the lowest recommended in the owner's manual.

On older cars, drop the collision coverage. This can save as much as $100 per year.

Drive as if there were an egg on the gas pedal. Fast starts consume vast amounts of gas.

Keep the car at 55 mph. It is a very economical speed.

In colder climates, don't forget to winterize. Check the battery; examine snow tires and chains; make sure all hoses are tight and the anti-freeze level is adequate.

Keep your car tuned up. Usually the best guide is found in your owner's manual. Read the guide and try to stick to the maintenance schedule. If you take good care of your car, there is no reason not to get 200,000 plus miles. (I have a newspaper clipping in my files about a Madison, Wisconsin, man who has a 1956 Cadillac Fleetwood limo with 903,756 miles. It still has the same engine with only one overhaul.)

Invest in some inexpensive tools and do some of your own work. A $3.00 investment can get you a car maintenance and repair guide that can save you many dollars.

On major repairs, get a written estimate. Make sure the estimate is specific on what is to be done and what limits are placed on additional "findings."

Keep all copies of work done in an envelope in the glove compartment. You'll find that this is a much better record than your memory.

Buying a car:

Consider a used car rather than a new one. Buy a car two years old (after it has depreciated 40% to 50% from the original sticker price) and drive it for at least three years before trading again.

Check the annual *Consumer Report* car survey. Each April, *Consumer Report* publishes the survey results of the reader's experience with a wide range of U.S. and foreign cars. CR also gives you a list of best buys by year and price range as well as "dogs" to avoid.

Look for:

Ripples in body panels or signs of repainting—this can mean body damage from an accident; worn foot pedals (or obviously new ones) can indicate hard use and high mileage; poor shock absorbers; "slushy" brake pedals; too much or too little play in the clutch pedal (1"); accessories that don't function properly; slow or sluggish starting and ragged running; bald tires; listen for noises while test driving.

Always have a garage mechanic check the car out before you decide to buy.

Recreation/Entertainment

Look for alternatives in family recreation. Rather than go to the movies, how about the zoo on family day? (Most locales have a time during the week where admission is free or greatly reduced.)

Take a camping vacation. This can be great fun and saves on expensive motel bills. Check around your church—many families have extra gear they would be willing to loan you.

If you do go to motels, go to ones that don't charge for children.

After the motel clerk gives you the rate on the type of room you ask for, inquire, "Do you have anything for less?" The clerk will always quote you the highest rate first, even though he has comparables for less. Location often causes a difference of up to $10 per day. For $10, I'll walk!

Go during "off" season if possible. A trip to Disneyland is much more expensive during the summer months than the off times. Many schools are going to year-round curriculums that provide breaks in mid-year. Everything—motels, meals, gas—is cheaper in off season.

Rather than go out for the evening, spend a family night at home. Let each member of the family choose a game or activity. Pop popcorn and get some pop and have a great time!

If you are driving a long distance, check with a local car dealer or finance company and see if you can arrange a "ferrying" job.

A tremendous activity can be a walk around your local area to really discover what is around you.

Food/Household

Generally, in season, buy fresh foods. Much savings can be gained by planting your own garden and picking your own fruit. If you grow your own produce, canning saves bundles!

On fresh fruits and vegetables, use a target price of seven cents per serving.

Shop at a cash-and-carry establishment—up to 25% savings is possible (mostly these are wholesale outlets, but they will sell to the general public).

Understand unit pricing. Get an inexpensive pocket calculator ($4.00 to $12.00) and carry it with you when you shop. This will allow you to compare the cost per ounce, pound, quart, etc., of competing items.

Use dry milk in recipes that call for milk.

Buy store brands.

Buy meat at the cost per serving.

Use your coupons! Buy a coupon wallet and carry it with you. Many stores now have coupon exchange baskets right in their store.

Cut down on the use of paper napkins, towels, and other disposables. Can you get by without them?

Avoid junk food. It has relatively little food value and is very expensive.

Unsweetened cereals are much less expensive than presweetened. They are better for you too.

Always use a written list when shopping and stick to it! This means you will have to plan your trip before you leave. Don't buy things on impulse; planning means saving.

Get to know the manager of the store you shop at, as well as heads of the meat department and produce department. These men know when certain items are going on sale and will be one of the best sources of savings information.

Do your own meat cutting! You'll still buy from the store, but instead of buying top round ($1.89 a lb.), bottom round ($1.89 a lb.) and eye-of-round ($2.39 a lb.), buy boneless round steak on sale ($1.09 a lb.) and cut your own. All you do is follow the little white line. To get more savings information like this, next time you're in the meat section, push the little buzzer and talk to the meat manager.

Make your own condiments and cleaners. There are many books and pamphlets (some free) telling you how to make mayonnaise, catsup, window cleaners, hand soap, etc., for a fraction of what you are paying in the store.

Use menu plans for the coming week. Key these to the weekly ads to get the lowest prices available. If something is a super buy, get a case, 50 pounds, etc. (make sure you have storage space).

Eat before you go shopping. If you go to the store hungry, it will cost you $7.48 more!

Keep your trip in each store to one-half hour. After one-half hour, fatigue sets in and you start buying at the clip of $1.00 per minute. Don't rush yourself so much, though, that you make rush decisions. This is where the advance planning above comes in (menu plans and complete lists).

Be careful on nonfood items. Sundries (toothpaste, shampoo, deodorant, etc.) are normally much more expensive in the grocery section than they will be in chain drugstores.

Tremendous savings can be had on baby food simply by investing in an inexpensive blender.

Check the reduced bins and close-out items.

Corn on the cob can be frozen. Corn is an excellent vegetable to plant in your garden or to buy when it reaches ten cents an ear.

Pie crust, baked rolls and biscuits are often on sale for ten cents to fifteen cents per tube (or right at one cent each). This is a good price to buy, but not at twenty-nine cents.

Beware of "sucker" sizes. These are 2½ lb. cans when most others are 3 lb. or 28 oz. instead of one quart.

Watch each item as it is rung up. Checkers make mistakes, especially on sale items. Be ready to correct any mistakes (either *for* or *against* you).

Clothes

Making your own clothing can be the biggest saver ever.

Don't hesitate to shop at Goodwill, Salvation Army, Union Gospel Mission, Disabled Veterans, etc. Some great buys are available here. (We have even found brand new clothes at these outlets at fantastic prices.)

Watch the clearance racks at stores. We have often purchased pants for the boys at ninety-nine cents a pair and dresses for the girls at fifty cents. If you're going to buy a sports coat for your pre-teenager, check the shops listed above first. (We can't justify paying $7.00 to $15.00 when we can get them for under $1.00.)

Shop garage sales and moving sales.

A good needle and thread can add years to your wardrobe. When sweaters wear out their elbows, sew on arm patches; they are quite economical and very stylish, while adding years of use to the sweater.

Factory seconds can be an outstanding bargain. Many textile mills also have outlet stores where tremendous bargains can be had on material.

Many larger localities have sample stores that have one-of-a-kind ready-mades on the rack. These are samples that were wholesaled to the dealers and can be obtained at savings up to 75%.

Furniture/Appliances

On appliances, study the manual that comes with it! It gives you valuable operational instructions as well as preventive maintenance ideas.

Used is beautiful!! Check the classifieds for moving sales or estate sales.

Invest in one or two inexpensive home maintenance and repair books. These are a tremendous source of little savings hints. Before calling in a repair man, check your manual and see if you can repair it yourself.

Basically, it will almost always be cheaper to repair something than it will be to go out and buy a new appliance. Don't hesitate to get several estimates.

The used furniture mentioned above will often need repairing. Usually reupholstering is cheaper than buying new furniture but check around! Sometimes furniture is being closed out and can be quite reasonable.

A good source of top-shaped (although usually lower quality) furniture can be a rental outfit. Once furniture has been in someone's home (sometimes only a few months) it can't be sold new. Don't hesitate to bargain; the worst they can say is no.

Check magazines like *Consumer Report* for comparisons of different models. Savings can be phenomenal!

Ceramic cooktops in electric units are a little more expensive, but very easy to clean. Also, when not in use, they can provide extra counter space.

Automatic ice cube maker costs about $50 extra, requires separate cold water line, takes up 1.5 cubic feet of freezer space. Is it worth it?

Top-loading washers usually take larger loads, require no stooping and don't need extra floor space for the door.

Cash purchases will always get you a better deal. Don't ever hesitate to bargain. Mark-up on most furniture is at least 50%, and can approach 500% on higher cost items.

Don't go for deluxe units. Normally all the extra dials, knobs and buttons don't add that much. I saw one mixer with 22 buttons. (I didn't even know that there were that many different names for mix.)

Always shop around. Spending a few extra days can save hundreds of dollars. Don't ever buy in a hurry.

Gifts

The best time to shop for gifts is any time during the year except the months of November and December. Get in the habit of buying all year. January clearance sales can be a great source of gifts for the next Christmas season.

Buy all year round. When you see good "stocking stuffers" on sale in July, buy them.

Have an inventory of wedding and shower gifts. All of us have been in a store when they have baby clothes or houseware items at fantastic prices (fifty cents for an outfit or bowls for ninety-nine cents). When you see these, buy one or two sets and put them aside for your next shower or wedding invitation.

Buy Christmas wrap, ribbon, decorations and cards in *Janu-*

ary. We have often purchased these items for ten cents on the dollar at this time of the year.

Make as many gifts as you can. I personally feel these are nicer than anything that can be bought. They show me that the person cared enough to spend something more valuable than money—they spent time.

Set a dollar limit per gift and stick to it. Because of the way we buy (clearance sales, close-outs, etc.), we often give gifts that would cost $10 to $20 cash. Our limit? $2.00!! (Still, as of 12/80.)

Don't ever charge gifts. If you go buying gifts without cash, you will invariably spend three to five times as much as you would if you spent cash, and the gift wouldn't be any nicer than those we give with our $2.00 limit!!

Don't give your children money to buy Christmas gifts, and don't buy them for them. Instead, begin in January to earn money for Christmas (we set 20% of earnings aside for gifts). As the children get older, design money-making projects to aid them in earning Christmas money. I used to sell Christmas cards and wrap from door-to-door. One of my favorite projects was selling large Baggies of mistletoe for fifty cents each. We used to make between $40 and $60 each selling door-to-door.

For ideas on over 100 jobs for kids, get *Training Your Children to Handle Money.*

Family Information

Date____________________

Full Name____
FIRST MIDDLE LAST

Address____
STREET OR RFD (COUNTY)

City____________ State____________ Zip Code____________ Telephone______

Date of Birth________________ Location of Birth Certificate________________

____

Social Security Number______________ Employer(s) last ten years:________________

____

____

Veteran?________ Service Number________ Veterans Administration Number__________

Disability, either service connected or nonservice connected?________________

Explain____

Single?________ Married?________ Widowed?________ Divorced?__________

Name of Spouse____

Address____
STREET OR RFD CITY STATE ZIP CODE

Date of Birth________________ Social Security Number________________

Children:

Full Names	Full Address	Date of Birth

What Do You Have To Will?
An Inventory of Your Estate

I. PERSONAL PROPERTY

A. Household furnishings, furniture, books, musical instruments, auto, etc.
List items for special consideration. Others may be grouped.

________________________________	$ ________
________________________________	$ ________
________________________________	$ ________
________________________________	$ ________
________________________________	$ ________
________________________________	$ ________
________________________________	$ ________
________________________________	$ ________
________________________________	$ ________

TOTAL APPROXIMATE VALUE $________

B. Cash (checking account)

Bank	Address	If Joint Account, With Whom?	Amount

TOTAL IN CHECKING ACCOUNTS $________

C. Cash (Savings Accounts)

Bank, Bld & Loan etc. Address	If Joint Account With Whom?	Amount

TOTAL IN SAVINGS ACCOUNTS $________

D. Stocks and Bonds (Government or other) If Joint

Item	Original Cost with Whom	Amount

TOTAL IN STOCKS AND BONDS $________

E. Money Invested in Mortgages and Personal Loans

Item	Address	Amount

TOTAL INVESTMENTS $________

TOTAL approximate
value of all PERSONAL PROPERTY (add items A, B, C, D, and E)

$________

Inventory continued

II. REAL PROPERTY (real estate and buildings)

Type of Property	Location	Original Cost	If Owned Jointly, With Whom?	Current Value

TOTAL APPROXIMATE VALUE OF REAL PROPERTY $________

III. Insurance

If the beneficiary of your life insurance policy should precede you in death, leaving no other beneficiary, the insurance would be payable to your estate, and therefore should be covered by your will.

Company	Owner of Policy	Beneficiary	Amount

TOTAL VALUE OF LIFE INSURANCE $________

TOTAL ASSETS (Add Personal Property, Real Property and Insurance)

$________

IV. APPROXIMATE DEBTS AND MORTGAGES AGAINST YOUR ESTATE

Debt or mortgage to whom?	Address	Amount

TOTAL APPROXIMATE INDEBTEDNESS $________

TOTAL APPROXIMATE VALUE OF ALL PERSONAL AND REAL PROPERTY AND INSURANCE! LESS TOTAL INDEBTEDNESS $________

How Do You Want Your Estate Distributed?

You do not need to describe every item of your personal or real property in your will—only if there is some specific item or piece of land that you want to go to a certain individual do you list it. And if you wish to name a specific sum of money to a person or organization, you will state the amount and the name.

Specific Bequests:

Person or Organization (Relationship)	Address	Item, Property or Sum of Money
(Christian Organization)		

After the specific bequests (if any) the simplest way to divide the residue of your estate is by percentages. Name the person or Christian organization you wish to remember, then state what percentage of the total remaining amount of your estate each is to receive.

Residue by Percentages:

Person or Organization (Relationship)	Address	Percentage
		%
		%
		%
		%

____________________ %

____________________ %

____________________ %

____________________ %

____________________ %

____________________ %

____________________ %

____________________ %

____________________ %

____________________ %

____________________ %

____________________ %

____________________ %

____________________ %

____________________ %

Keep Control—Name Your Personal Representative

A personal representative is one who is appointed by you to carry out the terms of your will. If you do not name a personal representative in your will, the court will appoint an administrator. He or she may not be one that you would have appointed, so exercise the right to name the person you want.

Due to unforeseen circumstances it would be well to name an alternate personal representative.

Name ____________ Relationship ____________ Alternate ____________ Relationship

Address ____________ Address

Protect Your Children—Name Their Guardian

If you have minor children, you should name a guardian for them in your will. This person will have charge of both the children and the property you have willed to them. You can narrow this service and have a guardian to care only for the children and a separate guardian or trustee for their estate. He or she will hold the property and expend it as the will directs.

Name of Guardian(s) ____________ Relationship ____________ Alternate Guardian(s) ____________ Relationship

Address ____________ Address

Name of Trustee ____________ Relationship ____________ Successor Trustee ____________ Relationship

Address ____________ Address

My Professional Advisors

My Minister	Name________	Street________ City________ State________
My Attorney	Name________	Street________ City________ State________
My Insurance Agent	Name________	Street________ City________ State________
My Accountant	Name________	Street________ City________ State________
My Banker or Trust Officer	Name________	Street________ City________ State________
My Broker	Name________	Street________ City________ State________
My tax records are Located	Name________	Street________ City________ State________
My safe deposit box is located	Name________	Street________ City________ State________
My will is located	Name________	Street________ City________ State________

For Further Information, Instructions or Questions

Your Signature ______________________________

Date ______________

Notes

WHOM DO I OWE?

		NAME	1 BALANCE	2 DUE DATE	3 INTEREST PERCENT	4 CONTRACT MONTHLY PAYMENT	5 PERCENT of TOTAL DUE	6 NEW BUDGET PAYMENT	
1									1
2									2
3									3
4									4
5									5
6									6
7									7
8									8
9									9
10									10
11									11
12									12
13									13
14									14
15									15
16									16
17									17

WHAT ARE MY RESOURCES?

	PAY 1	PAY 2	PAY 3	PAY 4
Gross Salary				
Federal W/H				
FICA				
State W/H				
Work Comp.				
Health Insurance				
Life Insurance				
Union Dues				
Retirement				
Other				
—				
—				
Net Pay				
Other Income				
—				
—				
—				
FUNDS AVAILABLE				

WHOM DO I OWE?

			NAME	1 BALANCE	2 DUE DATE	3 INTEREST PERCENT	4 CONTRACT MONTHLY PAYMENT	5 PERCENT of TOTAL DUE	6 NEW BUDGET PAYMENT	
1										1
2										2
3										3
4										4
5										5
6										6
7										7
8										8
9										9
10										10
11										11
12										12
13										13
14										14
15										15
16										16
17										17

WHAT ARE MY RESOURCES?

	PAY 1	PAY 2	PAY 3	PAY 4
Gross Salary				
Federal W/H				
FICA				
State W/H				
Work Comp.				
Health Insurance				
Life Insurance				
Union Dues				
Retirement				
Other				
—				
—				
Net Pay				
Other Income				
—				
—				
—				
FUNDS AVAILABLE				

BUDGET

		ITEM	1 IDEAL BUDGET (Monthly)	2 INTERIM BUDGET (Monthly)	3 CASH or CHECK per Pay Period	4 TO SAVINGS per Pay Period	
1		Savings 2 (Investments, etc.)					1
2		Tithe					2
3							3
4		Mortgage or Rent					4
5		Heat					5
6		Electricity					6
7		Water/Sewer					7
8		Garbage					8
9		Telephone					9
10		Car Insurance					10
11		Gasoline					11
12		Car Repairs					12
13		Recreation/Entertainment					13
14		Newspapers/Magazines					14
15		Health Insurance					15
16		Life Insurance					16
17		Doctors/Medical Expense					17

18	Food	18
19	Household	19
20	Cleaning/Dry Cleaning	20
21	Clothes	21
22	Home Furnishings	22
23	Contingencies	23
24	Christmas & Gifts	24
25	Vacation	25
26	Allowances	26
27	House Cleaning	27
28	Union Dues	28
29	Education	29
30		30
31		31
32		32
33		33
34		34
35	Debt Reduction (See attach.)	35
36		36
37	Total Expenses	37
38	Income Available	38
39	Other	39
40	Over/Short	40

BUDGET

	ITEM	1 IDEAL BUDGET (Monthly)	2 INTERIM BUDGET (Monthly)	3 CASH or CHECK per Pay Period	4 TO SAVINGS per Pay Period	
1	Savings 2 (Investments, etc.)					1
2	Tithe					2
3						3
4	Mortgage or Rent					4
5	Heat					5
6	Electricity					6
7	Water/Sewer					7
8	Garbage					8
9	Telephone					9
10	Car Insurance					10
11	Gasoline					11
12	Car Repairs					12
13	Recreation/Entertainment					13
14	Newspapers/Magazines					14
15	Health Insurance					15
16	Life Insurance					16
17	Doctors/Medical Expense					17

18		Food		18
19		Household		19
20		Cleaning/Dry Cleaning		20
21		Clothes		21
22		Home Furnishings		22
23		Contingencies		23
24		Christmas & Gifts		24
25		Vacation		25
26		Allowances		26
27		House Cleaning		27
28		Union Dues		28
29		Education		29
30				30
31				31
32				32
33				33
34				34
35		Debt Reduction (See attach.)		35
36				36
37		Total Expenses		37
38		Income Available		38
39		Other		39
40		Over/Short		40

BUDGETED PAYMENT PER PAY PERIOD

		1	2	3	4	5	6	
		Period 1	Period 2	Period 3	Period 4	Period 5	Period 6	
1	CASH:							1
2	Car Gas							2
3	Allowances/Cleaning							3
4	Food/Household							4
5	Entertainment							5
6								6
7	REGULAR CHECKS:							7
8	Mort./Rent							8
9	Heat							9
10	Electricity							10
11	Water/Sewer							11
12	Garbage							12
13	Telephone							13
14	Newspapers							14
15	Tithe							15
16	Medical Ins.							16
17	Union Dues							17

18			To Savings (1)		18
19			To Savings (2)		19
20			Debt Payments		20
21					21
22					22
23					23
24					24
25			Car Insurance		25
26			Magazines		26
27			Life Insurance		27
28			Car Repairs		28
29			Medical		29
30			Clothes		30
31			Furniture		31
32			Gifts		32
33			Vacation		33
34			Contingency		34
35			Education		35
36			Total Expenses		36
37			Income Available		37
38			From Savings		38
39			Other		39
40			Over/Short		40

BUDGETED PAYMENT PER PAY PERIOD

		Period 1	Period 2	Period 3	Period 4	Period 5	Period 6	
1	CASH:							1
2	Car Gas							2
3	Allowances/Cleaning							3
4	Food/Household							4
5	Entertainment							5
6								6
7	REGULAR CHECKS:							7
8	Mort./Rent							8
9	Heat							9
10	Electricity							10
11	Water/Sewer							11
12	Garbage							12
13	Telephone							13
14	Newspapers							14
15	Tithe							15
16	Medical Ins.							16
17	Union Dues							17

18	To Savings (1)	18
19	To Savings (2)	19
20	Debt Payments	20
21		21
22		22
23		23
24		24
25	Car Insurance	25
26	Magazines	26
27	Life Insurance	27
28	Car Repairs	28
29	Medical	29
30	Clothes	30
31	Furniture	31
32	Gifts	32
33	Vacation	33
34	Contingency	34
35	Education	35
36	Total Expenses	36
37	Income Available	37
38	From Savings	38
39	Other	39
40	Over/Short	40

BUDGETED PAYMENT PER PAY PERIOD

		Period 1	Period 2	Period 3	Period 4	Period 5	Period 6	
1	CASH:							1
2	Car Gas							2
3	Allowances/Cleaning							3
4	Food/Household							4
5	Entertainment							5
6								6
7	REGULAR CHECKS:							7
8	Mort./Rent							8
9	Heat							9
10	Electricity							10
11	Water/Sewer							11
12	Garbage							12
13	Telephone							13
14	Newspapers							14
15	Tithe							15
16	Medical Ins.							16
17	Union Dues							17

18	To Savings (1)	18
19	To Savings (2)	19
20	Debt Payments	20
21		21
22		22
23		23
24		24
25	Car Insurance	25
26	Magazines	26
27	Life Insurance	27
28	Car Repairs	28
29	Medical	29
30	Clothes	30
31	Furniture	31
32	Gifts	32
33	Vacation	33
34	Contingency	34
35	Education	35
36	Total Expenses	36
37	Income Available	37
38	From Savings	38
39	Other	39
40	Over/Short	40

BUDGETED PAYMENT PER PAY PERIOD

#		Period 1	Period 2	Period 3	Period 4	Period 5	Period 6	#
1	CASH:							1
2	Car Gas							2
3	Allowances/Cleaning							3
4	Food/Household							4
5	Entertainment							5
6								6
7	REGULAR CHECKS:							7
8	Mort./Rent							8
9	Heat							9
10	Electricity							10
11	Water/Sewer							11
12	Garbage							12
13	Telephone							13
14	Newspapers							14
15	Tithe							15
16	Medical Ins.							16
17	Union Dues							17

18	To Savings (1)	18
19	To Savings (2)	19
20	Debt Payments	20
21		21
22		22
23		23
24		24
25	Car Insurance	25
26	Magazines	26
27	Life Insurance	27
28	Car Repairs	28
29	Medical	29
30	Clothes	30
31	Furniture	31
32	Gifts	32
33	Vacation	33
34	Contingency	34
35	Education	35
36	Total Expenses	36
37	Income Available	37
38	From Savings	38
39	Other	39
40	Over/Short	40

BUDGETED PAYMENT PER PAY PERIOD

		Period 1	Period 2	Period 3	Period 4	Period 5	Period 6	
1	CASH:							1
2	Car Gas							2
3	Allowances/Cleaning							3
4	Food/Household							4
5	Entertainment							5
6								6
7	REGULAR CHECKS:							7
8	Mort./Rent							8
9	Heat							9
10	Electricity							10
11	Water/Sewer							11
12	Garbage							12
13	Telephone							13
14	Newspapers							14
15	Tithe							15
16	Medical Ins.							16
17	Union Dues							17

18			To Savings (1)		18
19			To Savings (2)		19
20			Debt Payments		20
21					21
22					22
23					23
24					24
25			Car Insurance		25
26			Magazines		26
27			Life Insurance		27
28			Car Repairs		28
29			Medical		29
30			Clothes		30
31			Furniture		31
32			Gifts		32
33			Vacation		33
34			Contingency		34
35			Education		35
36			Total Expenses		36
37			Income Available		37
38			From Savings		38
39			Other		39
40			Over/Short		40

BUDGETED PAYMENT PER PAY PERIOD

				1 Period 1	2 Period 2	3 Period 3	4 Period 4	5 Period 5	6 Period 6	
1			CASH:							1
2			Car Gas							2
3			Allowances/Cleaning							3
4			Food/Household							4
5			Entertainment							5
6										6
7			REGULAR CHECKS:							7
8			Mort./Rent							8
9			Heat							9
10			Electricity							10
11			Water/Sewer							11
12			Garbage							12
13			Telephone							13
14			Newspapers							14
15			Tithe							15
16			Medical Ins.							16
17			Union Dues							17

19	To Savings (2)	19
20	Debt Payments	20
21		21
22		22
23		23
24		24
25	Car Insurance	25
26	Magazines	26
27	Life Insurance	27
28	Car Repairs	28
29	Medical	29
30	Clothes	30
31	Furniture	31
32	Gifts	32
33	Vacation	33
34	Contingency	34
35	Education	35
36	Total Expenses	36
37	Income Available	37
38	From Savings	38
39	Other	39
40	Over/Short	40

BUDGETED PAYMENT PER PAY PERIOD

#		Period 1	Period 2	Period 3	Period 4	Period 5	Period 6	#
1	CASH:							1
2	Car Gas							2
3	Allowances/Cleaning							3
4	Food/Household							4
5	Entertainment							5
6								6
7	REGULAR CHECKS:							7
8	Mort./Rent							8
9	Heat							9
10	Electricity							10
11	Water/Sewer							11
12	Garbage							12
13	Telephone							13
14	Newspapers							14
15	Tithe							15
16	Medical Ins.							16
17	Union Dues							17

18	To Savings (1)	18
19	To Savings (2)	19
20	Debt Payments	20
21		21
22		22
23		23
24		24
25	Car Insurance	25
26	Magazines	26
27	Life Insurance	27
28	Car Repairs	28
29	Medical	29
30	Clothes	30
31	Furniture	31
32	Gifts	32
33	Vacation	33
34	Contingency	34
35	Education	35
36	Total Expenses	36
37	Income Available	37
38	From Savings	38
39	Other	39
40	Over/Short	40

BUDGETED PAYMENT PER PAY PERIOD

			1 Period 1	2 Period 2	3 Period 3	4 Period 4	5 Period 5	6 Period 6	
1		CASH:							1
2		Car Gas							2
3		Allowances/Cleaning							3
4		Food/Household							4
5		Entertainment							5
6									6
7		REGULAR CHECKS:							7
8		Mort./Rent							8
9		Heat							9
10		Electricity							10
11		Water/Sewer							11
12		Garbage							12
13		Telephone							13
14		Newspapers							14
15		Tithe							15
16		Medical Ins.							16
17		Union Dues							17

19	To Savings (2)	19
20	Debt Payments	20
21		21
22		22
23		23
24		24
25	Car Insurance	25
26	Magazines	26
27	Life Insurance	27
28	Car Repairs	28
29	Medical	29
30	Clothes	30
31	Furniture	31
32	Gifts	32
33	Vacation	33
34	Contingency	34
35	Education	35
36	Total Expenses	36
37	Income Available	37
38	From Savings	38
39	Other	39
40	Over/Short	40

BUDGETED PAYMENT PER PAY PERIOD

		Period 1	Period 2	Period 3	Period 4	Period 5	Period 6	
1	CASH:							1
2	Car Gas							2
3	Allowances/Cleaning							3
4	Food/Household							4
5	Entertainment							5
6								6
7	REGULAR CHECKS:							7
8	Mort./Rent							8
9	Heat							9
10	Electricity							10
11	Water/Sewer							11
12	Garbage							12
13	Telephone							13
14	Newspapers							14
15	Tithe							15
16	Medical Ins.							16
17	Union Dues							17

19	To Savings (2)	19
20	Debt Payments	20
21		21
22		22
23		23
24		24
25	Car Insurance	25
26	Magazines	26
27	Life Insurance	27
28	Car Repairs	28
29	Medical	29
30	Clothes	30
31	Furniture	31
32	Gifts	32
33	Vacation	33
34	Contingency	34
35	Education	35
36	Total Expenses	36
37	Income Available	37
38	From Savings	38
39	Other	39
40	Over/Short	40

SPENDING RECORD

DATE	CHECK #		DESCRIPTION		3 CONTRI-BUTIONS	4 SAVINGS	5 RENT OR MORT. PAYMENT	6 TRANS-PORTA-TION	7 RECREA-TION/ VACATN.	8 INSUR-ANCE
		1								
		2								
		3								
		4								
		5								
		6								
		7								
		8								
		9								
		10								
		11								
		12								

18	To Savings (1)	18
19	To Savings (2)	19
20	Debt Payments	20
21		21
22		22
23		23
24		24
25	Car Insurance	25
26	Magazines	26
27	Life Insurance	27
28	Car Repairs	28
29	Medical	29
30	Clothes	30
31	Furniture	31
32	Gifts	32
33	Vacation	33
34	Contingency	34
35	Education	35
36	Total Expenses	36
37	Income Available	37
38	From Savings	38
39	Other	39
40	Over/Short	40

SPENDING SUMMARY

ACCOUNT ______________________ BUDGET ______________________

			1	2	3	4	
	DATE	TRANSACTION		ALLOCA-TED	SPENT	BALANCE	
1							1
2							2
3							3
4							4
5							5
6							6
7							7
8							8
9							9
10							10
11							11
12							12
13							13
14							14
15							15
16							16

17		17
18		18
19		19
20		20
21		21
22		22
23		23
24		24
25		25
26		26
27		27
28		28
29		29
30		30
31		31
32		32
33		33
34		34
35		35
36		36
37		37
38		38

SPENDING SUMMARY

ACCOUNT BUDGET

	DATE	TRANSACTION	1	2 ALLOCATED	3 SPENT	4 BALANCE	
1							1
2							2
3							3
4							4
5							5
6							6
7							7
8							8
9							9
10							10
11							11
12							12
13							13
14							14
15							15
16							16

17		17
18		18
19		19
20		20
21		21
22		22
23		23
24		24
25		25
26		26
27		27
28		28
29		29
30		30
31		31
32		32
33		33
34		34
35		35
36		36
37		37
38		38

SPENDING SUMMARY

ACCOUNT BUDGET

	DATE	TRANSACTION	1	2 ALLOCA- TED	3 SPENT	4 BALANCE	
1							1
2							2
3							3
4							4
5							5
6							6
7							7
8							8
9							9
10							10
11							11
12							12
13							13
14							14
15							15
16							16

17	17
18	18
19	19
20	20
21	21
22	22
23	23
24	24
25	25
26	26
27	27
28	28
29	29
30	30
31	31
32	32
33	33
34	34
35	35
36	36
37	37
38	38

SPENDING SUMMARY

ACCOUNT ______ BUDGET ______

	DATE	TRANSACTION	1	2 ALLOCATED	3 SPENT	4 BALANCE	
1							1
2							2
3							3
4							4
5							5
6							6
7							7
8							8
9							9
10							10
11							11
12							12
13							13
14							14
15							15
16							16

17		17
18		18
19		19
20		20
21		21
22		22
23		23
24		24
25		25
26		26
27		27
28		28
29		29
30		30
31		31
32		32
33		33
34		34
35		35
36		36
37		37
38		38

SPENDING SUMMARY

ACCOUNT ______________________ BUDGET ______________________

			1	2	3	4	
	DATE	TRANSACTION		ALLOCATED	SPENT	BALANCE	
1							1
2							2
3							3
4							4
5							5
6							6
7							7
8							8
9							9
10							10
11							11
12							12
13							13
14							14
15							15
16							16

17		17
18		18
19		19
20		20
21		21
22		22
23		23
24		24
25		25
26		26
27		27
28		28
29		29
30		30
31		31
32		32
33		33
34		34
35		35
36		36
37		37
38		38

SPENDING SUMMARY

ACCOUNT ______________ BUDGET ______________

	DATE	TRANSACTION	1	2 ALLOCA-TED	3 SPENT	4 BALANCE	
1							1
2							2
3							3
4							4
5							5
6							6
7							7
8							8
9							9
10							10
11							11
12							12
13							13
14							14
15							15
16							16

17		17
18		18
19		19
20		20
21		21
22		22
23		23
24		24
25		25
26		26
27		27
28		28
29		29
30		30
31		31
32		32
33		33
34		34
35		35
36		36
37		37
38		38

SPENDING SUMMARY

ACCOUNT _______________ BUDGET _______________

	DATE	TRANSACTION	1	2 ALLOCATED	3 SPENT	4 BALANCE	
1							1
2							2
3							3
4							4
5							5
6							6
7							7
8							8
9							9
10							10
11							11
12							12
13							13
14							14
15							15
16							16

17		17
18		18
19		19
20		20
21		21
22		22
23		23
24		24
25		25
26		26
27		27
28		28
29		29
30		30
31		31
32		32
33		33
34		34
35		35
36		36
37		37
38		38

SPENDING SUMMARY

ACCOUNT ________________ BUDGET ________________

	DATE	TRANSACTION	1	2 ALLOCA-TED	3 SPENT	4 BALANCE	
1							1
2							2
3							3
4							4
5							5
6							6
7							7
8							8
9							9
10							10
11							11
12							12
13							13
14							14
15							15
16							16

17	18	19	20	21	22	23	24	25	26	27	28	29	30	31	32	33	34	35	36	37	38

SPENDING SUMMARY

ACCOUNT ______________________ BUDGET ______________________

	DATE	TRANSACTION	1	2 ALLOCA-TED	3 SPENT	4 BALANCE	
1							1
2							2
3							3
4							4
5							5
6							6
7							7
8							8
9							9
10							10
11							11
12							12
13							13
14							14
15							15
16							16

17		17
18		18
19		19
20		20
21		21
22		22
23		23
24		24
25		25
26		26
27		27
28		28
29		29
30		30
31		31
32		32
33		33
34		34
35		35
36		36
37		37
38		38

SPENDING SUMMARY

ACCOUNT BUDGET

	DATE	TRANSACTION	1	2 ALLOCATED	3 SPENT	4 BALANCE	
1							1
2							2
3							3
4							4
5							5
6							6
7							7
8							8
9							9
10							10
11							11
12							12
13							13
14							14
15							15
16							16

17		17
18		18
19		19
20		20
21		21
22		22
23		23
24		24
25		25
26		26
27		27
28		28
29		29
30		30
31		31
32		32
33		33
34		34
35		35
36		36
37		37
38		38

SPENDING SUMMARY

ACCOUNT

BUDGET

1 2 3 4

	DATE	TRANSACTION		ALLOCATED	SPENT	BALANCE	
1							1
2							2
3							3
4							4
5							5
6							6
7							7
8							8
9							9
10							10
11							11
12							12
13							13
14							14
15							15
16							16

17		17
18		18
19		19
20		20
21		21
22		22
23		23
24		24
25		25
26		26
27		27
28		28
29		29
30		30
31		31
32		32
33		33
34		34
35		35
36		36
37		37
38		38

SPENDING SUMMARY

ACCOUNT ______________________ BUDGET ______________________

	DATE	TRANSACTION	1	2 ALLOCATED	3 SPENT	4 BALANCE	
1							1
2							2
3							3
4							4
5							5
6							6
7							7
8							8
9							9
10							10
11							11
12							12
13							13
14							14
15							15
16							16

17		17
18		18
19		19
20		20
21		21
22		22
23		23
24		24
25		25
26		26
27		27
28		28
29		29
30		30
31		31
32		32
33		33
34		34
35		35
36		36
37		37
38		38

SPENDING SUMMARY

ACCOUNT

BUDGET

	DATE	TRANSACTION	1	2 ALLOCA-TED	3 SPENT	4 BALANCE	
1							1
2							2
3							3
4							4
5							5
6							6
7							7
8							8
9							9
10							10
11							11
12							12
13							13
14							14
15							15
16							16

17		17
18		18
19		19
20		20
21		21
22		22
23		23
24		24
25		25
26		26
27		27
28		28
29		29
30		30
31		31
32		32
33		33
34		34
35		35
36		36
37		37
38		38

SPENDING SUMMARY

ACCOUNT

BUDGET

	DATE	TRANSACTION	1	2 ALLOCA-TED	3 SPENT	4 BALANCE	
1							1
2							2
3							3
4							4
5							5
6							6
7							7
8							8
9							9
10							10
11							11
12							12
13							13
14							14
15							15
16							16

17		17
18		18
19		19
20		20
21		21
22		22
23		23
24		24
25		25
26		26
27		27
28		28
29		29
30		30
31		31
32		32
33		33
34		34
35		35
36		36
37		37
38		38

SPENDING SUMMARY

ACCOUNT BUDGET

	DATE	TRANSACTION	1	2 ALLOCATED	3 SPENT	4 BALANCE	
1							1
2							2
3							3
4							4
5							5
6							6
7							7
8							8
9							9
10							10
11							11
12							12
13							13
14							14
15							15
16							16

17		17
18		18
19		19
20		20
21		21
22		22
23		23
24		24
25		25
26		26
27		27
28		28
29		29
30		30
31		31
32		32
33		33
34		34
35		35
36		36
37		37
38		38

SPENDING SUMMARY

ACCOUNT BUDGET

	DATE	TRANSACTION	1	2 ALLOCA-TED	3 SPENT	4 BALANCE	
1							1
2							2
3							3
4							4
5							5
6							6
7							7
8							8
9							9
10							10
11							11
12							12
13							13
14							14
15							15
16							16

17		7
18		8
19		9
20		0
21		1
22		2
23		13
24		14
25		25
26		26
27		27
28		28
29		29
30		30
31		31
32		32
33		33
34		34
35		35
36		36
37		37
38		38

SPENDING SUMMARY

ACCOUNT BUDGET

	DATE	TRANSACTION	1	2 ALLOCATED	3 SPENT	4 BALANCE	
1							1
2							2
3							3
4							4
5							5
6							6
7							7
8							8
9							9
10							10
11							11
12							12
13							13
4							14
5							15
6							16

17 18 19 20 21 22 23 24 25 26 27 28 29 30 31 32 33 34 35 36 37 38

7 8 9 0 1 12 13 24 25 26 27 28 29 30 31 32 33 34 35 36 37 38

SPENDING SUMMARY

ACCOUNT ______________________ BUDGET ______________________

	DATE	TRANSACTION	1	2 ALLOCA-TED	3 SPENT	4 BALANCE	
1							1
2							2
3							3
4							4
5							5
6							6
7							7
8							8
9							9
10							10
11							11
12							12
13							13
14							14
15							15
16							16

17		17
18		18
19		19
20		20
21		21
22		22
23		23
24		24
25		25
26		26
27		27
28		28
29		29
30		30
31		31
32		32
33		33
34		34
35		35
36		36
37		37
38		38

SPENDING SUMMARY

ACCOUNT ______________________ BUDGET ______________________

	DATE	TRANSACTION	1	2 ALLOCA- TED	3 SPENT	4 BALANCE	
1							1
2							2
3							3
4							4
5							5
6							6
7							7
8							8
9							9
10							10
11							11
12							12
13							13
14							14
15							15
16							16

17		17
18		18
19		19
20		20
21		21
22		22
23		23
24		24
25		25
26		26
27		27
28		28
29		29
30		30
31		31
32		32
33		33
34		34
35		35
36		36
37		37
38		38

SPENDING SUMMARY

ACCOUNT ______ BUDGET ______

	DATE	TRANSACTION	1	2 ALLOCA-TED	3 SPENT	4 BALANCE	
1							1
2							2
3							3
4							4
5							5
6							6
7							7
8							8
9							9
10							10
11							11
12							12
13							13
14							14
15							15
16							16

17		17
18		18
19		19
20		20
21		21
22		22
23		23
24		24
25		25
26		26
27		27
28		28
29		29
30		30
31		31
32		32
33		33
34		34
35		35
36		36
37		37
38		38

SPENDING SUMMARY

ACCOUNT BUDGET

	DATE	TRANSACTION	1	2 ALLOCA-TED	3 SPENT	4 BALANCE	
1							1
2							2
3							3
4							4
5							5
6							6
7							7
8							8
9							9
10							10
11							11
12							12
13							13
14							14
15							15
16							16

17		17
18		18
19		19
20		20
21		21
22		22
23		23
24		24
25		25
26		26
27		27
28		28
29		29
30		30
31		31
32		32
33		33
34		34
35		35
36		36
37		37
38		38

SPENDING SUMMARY

ACCOUNT BUDGET

	DATE	TRANSACTION	1	2 ALLOCATED	3 SPENT	4 BALANCE	
1							1
2							2
3							3
4							4
5							5
6							6
7							7
8							8
9							9
10							10
11							11
12							12
13							13
14							14
15							15
16							16

17		17
18		18
19		19
20		20
21		21
22		22
23		23
24		24
25		25
26		26
27		27
28		28
29		29
30		30
31		31
32		32
33		33
34		34
35		35
36		36
37		37
38		38

SPENDING SUMMARY

ACCOUNT BUDGET

	DATE	TRANSACTION	1	2 ALLOCA- TED	3 SPENT	4 BALANCE	
1							1
2							2
3							3
4							4
5							5
6							6
7							7
8							8
9							9
10							10
11							11
12							12
13							13
14							14
15							15
16							16

17		17
18		18
19		19
20		20
21		21
22		22
23		23
24		24
25		25
26		26
27		27
28		28
29		29
30		30
31		31
32		32
33		33
34		34
35		35
36		36
37		37
38		38

SPENDING SUMMARY

ACCOUNT BUDGET

	DATE	TRANSACTION	1	2 ALLOCA-TED	3 SPENT	4 BALANCE	
1							1
2							2
3							3
4							4
5							5
6							6
7							7
8							8
9							9
10							10
11							11
12							12
13							13
14							14
15							15
16							16

17		17
18		18
19		19
20		20
21		21
22		22
23		23
24		24
25		25
26		26
27		27
28		28
29		29
30		30
31		31
32		32
33		33
34		34
35		35
36		36
37		37
38		38

SPENDING SUMMARY

ACCOUNT BUDGET

	DATE	TRANSACTION	1	2 ALLOCA-TED	3 SPENT	4 BALANCE	
1							1
2							2
3							3
4							4
5							5
6							6
7							7
8							8
9							9
10							10
11							11
12							12
13							13
14							14
15							15
16							16

17		17
18		18
19		19
20		20
21		21
22		22
23		23
24		24
25		25
26		26
27		27
28		28
29		29
30		30
31		31
32		32
33		33
34		34
35		35
36		36
37		37
38		38

SPENDING SUMMARY

ACCOUNT

BUDGET

	DATE	TRANSACTION	1	2 ALLOCA-TED	3 SPENT	4 BALANCE	
1							1
2							2
3							3
4							4
5							5
6							6
7							7
8							8
9							9
10							10
11							11
12							12
13							13
14							14
15							15
16							16

17		17
18		18
19		19
20		20
21		21
22		22
23		23
24		24
25		25
26		26
27		27
28		28
29		29
30		30
31		31
32		32
33		33
34		34
35		35
36		36
37		37
38		38

SPENDING SUMMARY

ACCOUNT ______________________ BUDGET ______________________

	DATE	TRANSACTION	1	2 ALLOCA-TED	3 SPENT	4 BALANCE	
1							1
2							2
3							3
4							4
5							5
6							6
7							7
8							8
9							9
10							10
11							11
12							12
13							13
14							14
15							15
16							16

17		17
18		18
19		19
20		20
21		21
22		22
23		23
24		24
25		25
26		26
27		27
28		28
29		29
30		30
31		31
32		32
33		33
34		34
35		35
36		36
37		37
38		38

SPENDING SUMMARY

ACCOUNT BUDGET

	DATE	TRANSACTION	1	2 ALLOCATED	3 SPENT	4 BALANCE	
1							1
2							2
3							3
4							4
5							5
6							6
7							7
8							8
9							9
10							10
11							11
12							12
13							13
14							14
15							15
16							16

17		17
18		18
19		19
20		20
21		21
22		22
23		23
24		24
25		25
26		26
27		27
28		28
29		29
30		30
31		31
32		32
33		33
34		34
35		35
36		36
37		37
38		38

SPENDING SUMMARY

ACCOUNT BUDGET

			1	2	3	4	
	DATE	TRANSACTION		ALLOCA-TED	SPENT	BALANCE	
1							1
2							2
3							3
4							4
5							5
6							6
7							7
8							8
9							9
10							10
11							11
12							12
13							13
14							14
15							15
16							16

17		17
18		18
19		19
20		20
21		21
22		22
23		23
24		24
25		25
26		26
27		27
28		28
29		29
30		30
31		31
32		32
33		33
34		34
35		35
36		36
37		37
38		38

SPENDING SUMMARY

ACCOUNT ______________________ BUDGET ______________________

	DATE	TRANSACTION	1	2 ALLOCA-TED	3 SPENT	4 BALANCE	
1							1
2							2
3							3
4							4
5							5
6							6
7							7
8							8
9							9
10							10
11							11
12							12
13							13
14							14
15							15
16							16

17		17
18		18
19		19
20		20
21		21
22		22
23		23
24		24
25		25
26		26
27		27
28		28
29		29
30		30
31		31
32		32
33		33
34		34
35		35
36		36
37		37
38		38

INSURANCE RECORD

				1	2	3	4	5	6	
			LIFE INSURANCE			INSURANCE AMOUNT	TOTAL ANNUAL PREMIUM	COMPANY & INSURANCE AGENT		
1										1
2										2
3										3
4										4
5										5
6										6
7			HEALTH INSURANCE							7
8			Health and Accident							8
9			Major Medical							9
10			Surgical							10
11			Disability							11
12			Other							12
13										13
14										14
15			HOUSE							15
16			Fire and Ext. Coverage							16

17	Liability	17
18	Living Expense	18
19	Wind and Water	19
20	Personal Property	20
21	Theft	21
22	Other	22
23		23
24		24
25	AUTO	25
26	Comprehensive	26
27	Collision	27
28	Bodily Injury	28
29	Property Damage	29
30	Medical	30
31	Fire and Theft	31
32	Other	32
33		33
34		34
35	OTHER	35
36		36
37		37
38		38